ECHOES OF NATURE: A BEAUTIFUL WILD HABITAT

NORTHWATER

CONSTANTINE ISSIGHOS

Copyright 2012 © Constantine Issighos. Published in Canada. Printed in U.S.A. No part of this book may be reproduced or transmitted in any form or by any means, electronic or mechanical, including photocopying, recording, and/or by any information storage and retrieval system except by a reviewer who may quote brief passages in a review to be printed in a magazine, newspaper, or on the web without written permission in writing from the author/publisher. For information, please contact www.awaqkunabooks.com

NorthWater is an imprint of Awaqkuna Books Inc.

Vol. 5 of THE AMAZON EXPLORATION SERIES:
ECHOES OF NATURE: A BEAUTIFUL WILD HABITAT

Library and Archives Canada

ISBN 978-0-9878599-4-5

Library and Archives Canada Cataloguing in Publication

ATTENTION CHILDRENS ASSOCIATIONS, BOOK STORES, PUBLIC OR PRIVATE LIBRARIES: quantity discounts are available on bulk purchases of this book series.

THE AMAZON EXPLORATION SERIES

Children's Books
by
Constantine Issighos

1. Upper Amazon Voyage by River Boat
2. The People of the River
3. The Children of the River
4. Amazon's Nature of Things
5. Echoes of Nature: a Beautiful Wild Habitat
6. The Amazon Rainforest
7. Amazonian Sisterhood
8. Amazon River Wolves
9. Amazonian Landscapes and Sunsets
10. Amazonian Canopy: the Roof of the World's Rainforest
11. Amazonian Tribes: a World of Difference
12. Birds and Butterflies of the Amazon
13. The Great Wonders of the Amazon
14. The Jaguar People
15. The Fresh Water Giants
16. The Call of the Shaman
17. Indigenous Families: Life in Harmony with Nature
18. Amazon in Peril
19. Giant Tarantulas and Centipedes

I am inviting you to share with me an adventure; alongside the tribes of the Amazon rainforest, a unique journey in which we can learn about how they hunt with spears or blowguns, their art and crafts, their ceremonies, their community and their harmonious relationship with wild nature.

The *Yanomani* Amazonian tribe are a culturally intact indigenous group, living in a *state of nature*, like the *Pirahas* tribe. They remain in an early state of nature by the fact that they have made little impact upon their environment, they have never discovered the wheel, and the only metal they use is what has been introduced to them by outside migrant settlers. Since they have lived in total isolation from the outside world, they have been able to maintain intact their customs and traditions. Their counting system begins with the number one, then two, and then just more than two. They are an original Amazon indigenous tribe whose roots date back more than 20,000 years. Their population is about 26,000 divided among 350 scattered villages in a territory the size of Austria, 98,000 square kilometres (38 square miles).

They are hunters and gatherers who have gained a superior balance and harmony with their Amazon environment. The *Yanomani* feast on all kinds of edible fare including bananas, avocados, sweet palm fruit, Brazil nuts, wild honey, insects, potatoes and cassava—also called manioc or yucca. They also hunt and consume the wild meat of small animals, fish, frogs, wild pigs and snakes. By our western standards, the *Yanomani* enjoy a high rate of nutrient and protein intake. Much of their food comes from their gardens; they eat more fruits and vegetables than wild meat.

Now that we have gotten over the preliminary statistical information of one of the many Amazonian tribes, let's us turn our attention to a broader subject that will include 98% of the social and cultural structure of the indigenous people living in the Amazon of South America. Of course, when we are viewing indigenous tribes, there are always the exceptions, but this exception does not affect the rule of similarity.

Indigenous Amazonians have lived in this diversified environment for many centuries. They all have developed their own distinctive ways of life in harmony with nature and the practice of communally sharing their hunt and the food they gather. Most of the tribesmen believe in reincarnation, that they will reborn through their grandchildren.

Many indigenous live in communal homes where all members form an extended family. In such a communal culture, the indigenous people help and protect each other to make it through life, and *sharing* is a key factor to survival, as the community does not tolerate misers or laziness. Each extended family home or village considers itself an autonomous socio-economic entity—*yamaki*—we the co-residents. Their members prefer to marry within their community with a "cross" cousin, the son or daughter of a maternal uncle or paternal aunt.

These kinds of marriage unions are repeated as often as possible between the extended families or villagers in a generation; from generation to generation they form a collective bond among their members.

This does not mean that villages or extended families live in isolation. All local groups maintain a social network of matrimonial, ceremonial and socio-economic reciprocal relations with various nearby groups considered friendly. This links and maintains the totality of the tribal collective cohesiveness from one end of the tribal territory to the other.

These kinds of communal attributes are celebrated with ceremonies. By dressing up in colourful costumes, they give thanks for the year's harvest or to the spirits that protect the entire community. In theses ceremonies, the spiritual shaman—witch doctor—circles, chanting, blowing tobacco smoke and stroking people with flowers. The bundle of flowers is then taken and buried in the forest so that the spirits will not be disturbed and others will not be affected by it. When this is done, no curse can work against the people attending the ceremonies and the evil is removed.

An indigenous community has no formal leader, but every extended family has a chief who stands up for the interests of his family. There is also the shaman who is more powerful than the chiefs; he heals diseases, gives protection against bad demons and solves disputes. If there is a dispute between different families that cannot be settled, then families tend to move on and form their own village.

Indigenous spirituality is divided into the good spirits and the bad spirits. Each of these manifests their presence in the world of humans in different ways. The shaman acts as a mediator between humans and different levels of spirits. With the help of medicinal plants, the shaman seeks to communicate with the good spirits and combat the demonic forces, although the shaman may also use his power at the service of demons to defeat his own or the village's real or imaginary enemies.

Life in indigenous villages is far from ideal, for such an "ideal-life" does not exist anywhere on earth. But the people's relationship to the natural environment is healthy and it is reflected in their daily attitude and practices towards it. No food is wasted from the wild habitat of the Amazon rainforest.

Following is a structural description of a typical indigenous village where this harmonious interaction takes place. A clearing made by humans in the middle of the rainforest indicates the presence of an indigenous village or of an extended family compound. This clearing is made up of sections arranged in concentric circles. The largest structure is the communal house, located in the center, which is the focal point of village life, and where most of the social activities are held.

It has a living capacity for about 60 to 80 people, with an overall diameter of 10-12 meters (30-36 feet). One of its internal divisions is made up of a circular section where the main kitchen is located and where the communal meals are cooked. It also serves as a visiting area and where festivals are held. At night it becomes the sleeping quarters for the young bachelor men. A secondary round space is further divided into walled compartments for single families of the extended family.

Surrounding the communal house there is an outdoor space which women use as a meeting place and which can also be used for outdoor festivals.

In the spatial organization of the village there also the work houses, one per extended family. These are small rectangular houses with no walls and with a palm leaf roof of two slopes. These houses are mainly used by women to scrape manioc, cook, sew and weave. Men use the space to fix their hunting and fishing tools.

Adjacent to the village's perimeter are small gardening plots, one per extended family, where women cultivate and harvest vegetables, tobacco, cotton, sugarcane and medicinal plants. In this way the indigenous women maintain their food traditions and the methods of producing these foods. Women produce more than 30% of the food consumed in the family; men do the hunting, fishing and gathering. The gardens or small fields mark the end of the village's land. In the distance one can see other man-made clearings that mark the neighbouring village.

The indigenous people of the Amazon live in many different wild ecological environments and they have adapted their communal structure and culture to these diversified areas. Due to the diversified wild nature of the Amazon rainforest, most indigenous tribes exist in the grasslands by the riverbanks, the pampas (valleys), while some others live in semi-desert areas.

Tribes that live by the Amazon River basin tend to dedicate themselves to fishing and the construction of dugout canoes. Dugout canoes are made from a single huge tree; its center is fire-burned, dug out and shaped into a large canoe. The dugout canoes are used as a means of transportation and communication with other tribes or to seek a shaman's medicinal remedies.

The Amazon tribes are, therefore, attuned to live in harmony with their wild habitat and with the ecological realities of the climate i.e., river-floods and strong rainstorms. This is the result of 5,000 years of experimentation and accumulated knowledge, giving them a strong understanding of how to manage their wild habitat. They meet their needs according to sustainable requirements, not through marketing principles. They see the importance of maintaining a balanced biodiversity through the careful allocation of cultivated fields and natural forests to be occupied by wild species of special interest to them.

If the Amazon rainforest seems a "far-too-far-off" exotic place from where we are, let's see how surprisingly close we are to the products that come from there. Take an imaginary trip with me into the Amazon rainforest and take a look around you! What do you see that is familiar? Do you see that most of the natural things we enjoy in our homes come from the rainforests of the world? Among these natural things are 120 pharmaceutical drugs (that prevent or cure diseases), chocolate, cocoa, sugar, pineapples, bamboo, rubber and yucca, as well as, important spices such as ginger, cinnamon, turmeric, paprika, and vanilla. This is the proper way to envisage our relationship with the Amazon rainforest and to recognize the importance it plays in our lives.

I could not end this article about the beautiful, wild Amazonian habitat without describing its spectacular sunsets. At some point during my long riverbank walks, I closed my eyes and leaned against the trunk of an old *Kapok* tree. The glow from the end of my torch matched the sunset ahead of me.

I was nearing the end of my voyage to the Amazon River. I had to admit that there was something special about ending my journey while looking at the beautiful sunset that nature had unveiled before me had found myself watching the sunsets recently, contemplating the way my journey was ending. The sunsets had a calming effect on me, and soothed my uneasy thoughts about leaving the many people I had met, spoken to, photographed and come to deeply appreciate.

The rainy season had cast a bright orange haze above the canopy's horizon, illuminating the sky as if lit by fire, yet the sky above the haze was crisp and clear. I continued to lean on the kapok tree for a time, then walked down the grassy path and ducked underneath the thick vines hanging from the densely spaced trees towards my camp. A cool evening breeze arose, making me stop in the middle of the path. I looked at the sunset, once again now visible behind the trees. It seemed to stare at me, a bright orange orb of wonderment that was the very thing that gave me a sense of peace and life-giving light. I was so grateful for having had this one in a lifetime opportunity to visit and live for a few months in this beautiful wild habitat like no other on earth!

ASHANINKAS INDIANS

The great majority of the Ashaninkas live in Peru; the rest live in the Brazilian territories. They are considered a "warrior-tribe" due to their historical struggle against incursions of their land by loggers, miners and rubber companies.

The "internal armed conflict" in the 1980's severely affected the Ashaninkas; thousands were displaced, others were killed or just disappeared. In 2003 the Ashaninkas of Peru were finally granted Communal Reserve rights to their ancestral lands.

Since 2003 the Ashaninkas have been rebuilding their fractured society, creating and developing projects to protect their land and documenting and archiving its use so they will have a greater say in its conservation and ecologically sustainability.

The Ashaninkas spiritual characteristics–that make up their shamanic cosmology–are divided between the existences of the visible world and an invisible world behind this visible world.

The shaman is the mediator between the invisible and the visible worlds. The special nature of the Ashaninkas resides in their dualistic conception of a universe with clearly defined boundaries between good and evil.

The Amazonian city of Iquitos is famous as a bird-watching destination.

Birding can be done in a diversity of habitats like a bamboo forest, a flood plain, a hill forest or a swamp, all within a short distance from the city. Without doubt, the most beautiful and prized species of parrots in the world can be found here.

The popularity and desirability of Parrots in the Upper Amazon is due to their rarity in the world, their beautiful adorned plumage, and their talking ability. Popularized by the recent discovery of new species of birds as well as isolated populations of quite a few other enigmatic birds, birding here can be a slow pursuit.

While birding is slow here, what you see is typically high quality. Several sites can be visited along 25 to 35 km of the Iquitos-Nauta road.

Among the most intelligent of birds; the Amazon Parrot is a bird worthy of a place in the aviary of any person with the facility and time to keep such a beautiful species.

The Amazon Exploration Series *Constantine Issighos*

Echoes of Nature: A Beautiful Wild Habitat

The Amazon Exploration Series *Constantine Issighos*

Echoes of Nature: A Beautiful Wild Habitat

www.ingramcontent.com/pod-product-compliance
Lightning Source LLC
Chambersburg PA
CBHW041755040426
42446CB00001B/36